Contents

FOREWORD

WHO WHEN Community Colleges Now

Two years ago, the American Association of Community Colleges (AACC) and its 21st-Century Commission on the Future of Community Colleges issued a bold call to action: If community colleges are to contribute powerfully to meeting the needs of 21st-century students and the 21st-century economy, education leaders must reimagine what these institutions are—and are capable of becoming.

At that time, the Commission's report, *Reclaiming the American Dream: Community Colleges and the Nation's Future*, set a goal of increasing rates for completion of community college credentials (certificates and associate degrees) by 50% by 2020, while preserving access, enhancing quality, and eradicating attainment gaps across groups of students. The report set forth seven major recommendations, all of which are connected to attaining that goal.

Now AACC's 21st-Century Initiative moves from idea to action. The implementation guidelines presented here provide a blueprint for colleges and others to implement the seven recommendations—to **redesign** students' educational experiences, **reinvent** institutional roles, and **reset** the system so it better promotes student success.

Each year, community colleges enroll about 12.7 million students in credit and noncredit courses.[1] These institutions typically serve every student who walks through their doors. They provide the gateway to higher education for students who may never have even dreamed of going to college.

But access alone is no longer sufficient. A highly educated population is essential for economic growth and a strong democracy. Yet completion rates in U.S. higher education have stagnated. While more students are starting college, too few students are completing credentials.

Community colleges cannot be strong by being the same. Certain values remain constant: opportunity, equity, academic excellence. But as the Commission report asserts, if community colleges are to enact those values in the 21st century, *"virtually everything else must change"* (p. 20). Taking on bold ideas and dramatic change is the only way to meet college completion goals.

The coming work is no doubt challenging—for community colleges and for the education, policy, and business communities that will partner with and support them. But this ongoing effort is clearly required to ensure that community colleges live up to their promise to help reclaim the American Dream.

Walter G. Bumphus
President and CEO
American Association of Community Colleges

Build A Blueprint for Change

Restoring the middle class—and global competitiveness

Community colleges are vibrant hubs of aspiration, learning, and workforce training. They open their doors to everyone willing to enter and provide an affordable education to almost half of all the undergraduate students in the United States.

For many students, particularly those who have not been well served by their prior education, community colleges provide an educational home that can launch a lifetime of success. However, the United States is not yet enjoying the full benefit community colleges might contribute in terms of strengthening the nation's workforce, building a healthier and more competitive economy, and sustaining a vital, inclusive democracy.

Realizing these national economic and social objectives depends in large part on significantly increasing college completion—and community colleges must play a pivotal role in attaining that widely embraced but challenging goal.

The 2012 report *Reclaiming the American Dream: Community Colleges and the Nation's Future* examined a range of educational and economic data, recognized that too few students are leaving community colleges with credentials and career-ready skills, and found great potential for improvement. The report concluded that community colleges are at a crossroads of challenge and opportunity.

Challenge. The United States is falling behind other countries in terms of educational attainment. After generations of leading the world in college degree completion, the U.S. now ranks 16th in college completion rates for 25- to 34-year-olds.[2] Median income in the United States stagnated between 1972 and 2000—and since 2000, it has declined by 7%.[3] A child born poor in the United States today is more likely to remain poor than at any time in U.S. history,

the middle class is shrinking,[4] income inequality is rising, and the American promise that each generation will do better than the last is under threat.

Opportunity. By 2018, nearly two-thirds of all American jobs will require a postsecondary certificate or degree, and that means adding 15–20 million educated employees to the workforce by 2025.[5] These employees can be—should be—the heart of a reinvigorated middle class, people for whom a college credential means the difference between a dead-end, low-wage job and a career that can support a family. Where will these new employees be educated? Most likely at community colleges.

Community colleges are the gateway to higher education for the students who can be tomorrow's middle class. Research has indicated that 20% of students at four-year institutions had family incomes below $32,000, compared with 28% at two-year institutions and 65% at less-than-two-year institutions.[6]

Data from community colleges underscore a dramatic need for improved completion rates. Fewer than half (46%) of students who enter community colleges with the goal of earning a degree or certificate have attained that goal, have transferred to a baccalaureate institution, or are still enrolled six years later.[7]

If community colleges take bold action to improve college completion, they not only will better serve their students, but they also can help rebuild the U.S. workforce and improve its global competitiveness—and address income inequality, reverse the decline of the U.S. middle class, and restore the promise of the American Dream.

AACC's 21st-Century Initiative

The American Association of Community Colleges (AACC) launched its 21st-Century Initiative to drive the transformation community colleges need to dramatically improve college completion.

The 21st-Century Initiative began with a listening tour that gathered ideas from students, college faculty and staff, administrators, trustees, state policymakers, and college presidents and chancellors across the country. Then the 21st-Century Commission on the Future of Community Colleges—using findings from the listening tour and safeguarding fundamental values of open access, equity, and excellence—began to envision a new future for community colleges.

The Commission's report, *Reclaiming the American Dream: Community Colleges and the Nation's Future,* set the goal of increasing rates for completion of community college credentials (associate degrees and certificates) by 50% by 2020. The Commission also concluded that the only way to attain this goal is to transform community colleges—to **redesign** students' educational experiences, **reinvent** institutional roles, and **reset** the system so it better promotes student success. The report set forth seven recommendations to drive this transformation.

- **Recommendation 1:** Increase completion rates by 50% by 2020

- **Recommendation 2:** Dramatically improve college readiness

- **Recommendation 3:** Close the American skills gap

- **Recommendation 4:** Refocus the community college mission and redefine institutional roles

- **Recommendation 5:** Invest in collaborative support structures

- **Recommendation 6:** Target public and private investments strategically

- **Recommendation 7:** Implement policies and practices that promote rigor and accountability

With this *Implementation Guide*, the 21st-Century Initiative takes another step forward. AACC convened nine implementation teams to identify strategies and resources that colleges can use in work to implement the seven recommendations. The teams, composed of community college experts and former commissioners, reviewed pertinent research, examined work already underway, and identified challenges to moving forward.

This *Implementation Guide* is the result of their efforts. It outlines specific actions colleges can take—must take—to address the challenges and improve completion rates.

The guide is written primarily for community college administrators, faculty, staff, and governing board members, with student success top of mind. However, individuals and organizations in the education, policy, and business communities also will play important collaborative roles in designing, implementing, and supporting many of the recommended actions.

To help all of these parties do this critical work, AACC has established an online 21st-Century Center. This online center highlights emerging research, new examples of college and system work, and initiatives undertaken by AACC and other national community college organizations. Visit www.aacc21stcenturycenter.org.

The typical ways of educating community college students are not working well enough. Everyone concerned with improving outcomes must reconsider community college roles, structures, and approaches. Colleges must rethink and reshape every aspect of their work—policy frameworks, programs of study, student support, and relationships with those around them—with one goal in mind: giving community college students the tools, motivation, and support to finish what they start.

Move From Idea to Implementation

Key Strategies for Change

This *Implementation Guide* is organized by the seven recommendations that must drive the transformation of community colleges. However, there are four foundational strategies that are addressed in multiple recommendations:

- Clear, coherent academic/career pathways (explained on page 11)

- Stackable credentials based on clearly defined competencies (explained on page 21)

- Alignment of learning across education sectors, within community colleges, and with labor-market demands (explained on page 26)

- Transparency and accountability (explained on page 34)

Each of these strategies can not only increase the number of postsecondary credentials awarded, but also strengthen the link between credentials and employment. Each can help ensure that every student has a viable route to a certificate, a degree, a first job, further education, and career advancement.

Most community colleges already use some or all of these strategies in limited ways, typically for technical and professional careers like nursing. However, there is no reason that other disciplines and entire institutions cannot use these approaches—except that they often require a break from the way things have always been done. It is time for community colleges to set aside the *usual* way and invest in a *better* way for all students in all programs of study.

Implementation With Purpose

A redesigned model for education is only as good as its implementation. Thus, whatever strategies colleges adopt, they must be mindful of the quality of implementation—how new models are designed, who is involved, and whether data inform decision making. Colleges that implement effectively follow the tenets below.

- **Commit to the work.** Sustainable change requires the commitment and persistent focus of all involved parties.

- **Use and share data.** Data and research—about student characteristics and progress, educational effectiveness, and institutional performance—are essential for informed decision making, and they must be shared across K–12 and postsecondary levels.

- **Design for scale.** Experience of the past decade amply demonstrates that well-intentioned and well-executed interventions do not produce significant improvements if they are implemented only for small numbers of students.

- **Embrace diversity.** Colleges cannot create conditions conducive to improved learning for all students unless they understand diverse students and eliminate institutional barriers to their success.

- **Integrate technology creatively.** Colleges must strike the balance between using technology when it provides superior tools—for example, in sharing data, monitoring progress, delivering certain kinds of information, and enriching learning—and building human connections.

- **Emphasize professional development.** Professional development for faculty, staff, administrators, and governing board members should be expected, strategically focused, and adequately supported.

- **Prepare new leaders.** Leaders ready for the future are open to new institutional roles and structures, comfortable with data, capable of leading transformational change, and relentlessly focused on equity and student success.

- **Focus governing board work.** Substantial improvement depends significantly on boards taking seriously their responsibility to create the policy conditions necessary to improve student progress and success—beginning with hiring the CEO who will lead transformational change and supporting her or him in doing courageous work.

Increase completion rates by 50% by 2020

Increase completion rates of students earning community college credentials (certificates and associate degrees) by 50% by 2020, while preserving access, enhancing quality, and eradicating attainment gaps associated with income, race, ethnicity, and gender.

To meet the challenge of dramatically increasing college completion rates, community colleges will have to fundamentally redesign students' educational experiences.

How Can Colleges Do This Work?

Advice to colleges focuses on six implementation strategies:

- **Publicly commit to explicit goals for college completion.** At the institution and state levels, articulate aggressive numeric goals, time frames, and the commitment to achieve equity in outcomes for a diverse student population.

- **Create pathways.** Construct coherent, structured pathways to certificate and degree completion, and then ensure that students enter a pathway soon after beginning college.

- **Expand prior-learning assessments.** Maximize appropriate awards of college credits for prior learning, such as learning acquired through military service.

- **Devise completion strategies on both ends of the college experience.** Improve student outcomes in high-risk entry-level classes, such as college-prep algebra and college-level mathematics, and help students who have completed 30 credit hours take the final steps toward completion.

- **Establish guarantees for seamless transfer.** Advocate state policy that ensures transfer of designated courses, certificates, and degrees from community colleges to universities and monitors compliance.

- **Implement automatic graduation and reverse transfer programs.** Ensure that students who transfer before completing an associate degree are awarded credit toward community college credentials for courses completed at other community colleges and baccalaureate institutions.

Work Underway: Strategies for Increasing Graduation Rates

The national community college organizations— AACC, Achieving the Dream (ATD), Association of Community College Trustees (ACCT), Center for Community College Student Engagement *(CCCSE)*, League for Innovation in the Community College, and Phi Theta Kappa (PTK)—have committed to an array of strategies aimed at dramatically increasing college completion rates. Many of these strategies involve significant collaboration. Examples of this work include the following:

- **AACC** is showcasing the excellent work of numerous membership, research, and philanthropic organizations through its online 21st-Century Center.

- **ACCT** has brought urgency and focus to the role of trustees through its annual student success symposium and through the Governance Institutes for Student Success conducted in partnership with **Student Success Initiatives** at The University of Texas at Austin.

- **ATD,** working with an expanding national network (currently more than 200 colleges), focuses on transformational change for student success and equity.

- *CCCSE*, which works with colleges across the country, is producing a series of reports focused on issues colleges must address to attain completion goals—bringing high-impact educational practices to scale; improving outcomes for men of color; and strengthening the role of part-time faculty.

- **PTK** is expanding the high-impact, student-led Community College Completion Corps (C4) campaign and collaborates with *CCCSE* on getting messages to students about ways to strengthen their prospects for success.

- **AACC** and the **League for Innovation in the Community College** are undertaking new leadership development initiatives because bold and visionary leadership is requisite to achieving the goal set for community college completion.

At the state system and college levels, the following are examples of strategies to increase graduation rates:

Publicly commit to explicit goals for college completion

- At **William Rainey Harper College (IL),** leaders ask a simple question: "What's your number?" For Harper, the number is 10,604 additional graduates by 2020, with specific targets set for each year.

- In **North Carolina,** the **State Board of Community Colleges** established SuccessNC with a specific goal of increasing the percentage of students who transfer, complete credentials, or remain continuously enrolled after six years. The baseline is 45% for the fall 2004 cohort, and the goal is a six-year success rate of 59% for the fall 2014 cohort. Reaching this target will double the number of credential completers by 2020. This work was done in collaboration with leaders from the **North Carolina Association of Community College Presidents** and **North Carolina Association of Community College Trustees.**

Expand prior-learning assessments

- College Credit for Heroes, a **Texas Partner Community Colleges** project, identifies, develops, and supports methods to maximize the awarding of college credits for military educational experiences. The program emphasizes accelerated degree and certificate completion to expedite veterans' entry into the workforce.

Devise completion strategies on both ends of the college experience

- **City University of New York** community colleges have produced impressive results—doubling associate degree completion rates for participants in their Accelerated Student in Associate Programs initiative. Students are grouped in cohorts according to selected majors, and they have consolidated schedules in morning, afternoon, or evening time frames, along with intensive support.

Establish guarantees for seamless transfer

- **Tennessee Transfer Pathways** serve as advising tools and reflect an agreement between the state's community colleges and four-year colleges/universities. Students who complete all the designated courses in a particular Transfer Pathway earn an associate degree at the community college, and pathway completion is documented on their transcripts. Upon transfer, students are guaranteed that all the pathway courses taken at the community college will be accepted at the college/university and will count toward completion of the applicable major.

Implement automatic graduation and reverse transfer programs

- At the end of each term, **Seminole State College (FL)** conducts degree audits on students in career programs who have completed capstone courses. Students who have completed certificate or associate programs are then awarded the credential and notified of their success.

- The strong partnership between **El Paso Community College (TX)** and the University of Texas at El Paso (UTEP) features an automatic reverse transfer system. Students who transfer to UTEP with at least 25% of an associate degree completed are tracked and then notified when they have earned enough credit to be awarded an associate degree.

Multiple strategies

- With support from The Kresge Foundation, statewide **Student Success Centers** have been established in **Arkansas, California, Connecticut, Michigan, New Jersey, Ohio**, and **Texas.** These centers organize a state's community colleges around common action. Together, they work to accelerate institutional and state policy change—all in support of student success at scale.

Where Can Colleges Learn More?

- Completion by Design is a five-year initiative with a goal of significantly increasing completion and graduation rates for low-income students up to age 25. Its website includes a Knowledge Center and Toolkits: www.completionbydesign.org and www.completionbydesign.org/our-approach/step-3-diagnose-the-issues/pathway-analyses-toolkit

- Complete College America describes features of *Guided Pathways to Success:* www.completecollege.org/docs/GPS_Summary_FINAL.pdf

- Jobs for the Future describes statewide student success centers: www.jff.org/publications/joining-forces-how-students-success-centers-are-accelerating-statewide-community

PATHWAYS

- Dadgar, M., Venezia, A., Nodine, T., & Bracco, K. R. (2013). *Providing structured pathways to guide students toward completion.* San Francisco: WestEd.

- Jenkins, D., & Cho, S. (2012). *Get with the program: Accelerating community college students' entry into and completion of programs of study* [CCRC Working Paper No. 32]. New York: Community College Research Center, Teachers College, Columbia University.

- Karp, M. M. (2013). *Entering a program: Helping students make academic and career decisions* [CCRC Working Paper No. 59]. New York: Community College Research Center, Teachers College, Columbia University.

- McClenney, K., & Dare, D. (2013, June/July). *Forging new academic pathways: Reimagining the community college experience with students' needs and best interests at heart.* Community College Journal, 21–26.

- McClenney, K., Dare, D., & Thomason, S. (2013, April/May). *Premise and promise: Developing new pathways for community college students.* Community College Journal, 56–63.

THE PATHWAY: A STRUCTURED EDUCATIONAL EXPERIENCE

A pathway is a highly structured, coherent educational experience that is built around and through an area of study. Whenever the student enters college—directly after high school or as an adult returning to education—the student's experience includes development of a clear academic plan, a defined learning sequence, engagement in high-impact educational practices, built-in advising and other student support, integrated hands-on and co-curricular learning, and a clear route to transfer and/or employment. Increasingly, a pathway will encompass multiple majors in related fields, crossing traditional boundaries between programs in technical/professional fields and those in the arts and sciences.

The pathway is a partnership between the student and the institution, with clearly defined expectations for both parties. It provides the framework for the college's interaction with the student, starting with the initial point of contact, which may be as early as middle or high school.

At entry, the student's skills and strengths are assessed, and the student is matched with the institutional resources (e.g., academic skills brush-up, advising, and financial aid) that he or she needs to achieve his or her stated goals. As part of this process, the student develops a clearly articulated educational plan and enters a pathway as soon as possible following college entry, likely choosing among several pathway options. The student's decision is informed by clear information, provided by the college, about employment opportunities and potential earnings associated with each pathway.

Successful navigation of the pathway is supported through integrated academic and student support services. The pathway includes periodic checkpoints with interventions that help keep the student on track, circumvent failure, and provide opportunities to celebrate success. It also reflects careful articulation across levels of study, from point of entry through attainment of a postsecondary credential, transfer to a baccalaureate program, career entry, and job placement or advancement. Finally, the pathway ensures that the student's credentials are aligned with business and industry requirements.

PATHWAY MILESTONES

The pathway is a partnership between the college and its students. In the pathway model, students have four major milestones, and the college's actions can help students through each one.

- **CONNECTION:** the connection between high school and community college, or from interest to application.

- **ENTRY:** the period from enrollment to the completion of core courses.

- **PROGRESS:** the time from entry into a program of study to completion of 75% of requirements.

- **COMPLETION:** completion of a credential with value in the labor market.

COLLEGE ACTIONS BY MILESTONE

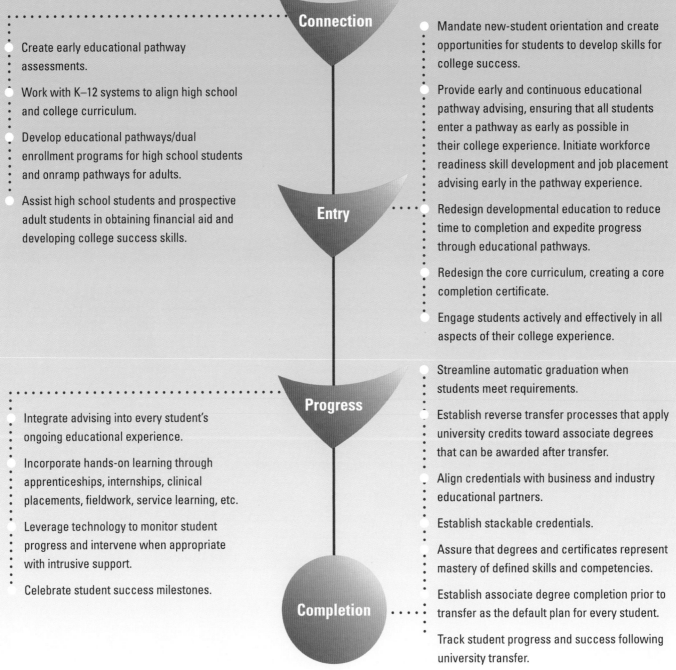

Connection

- Create early educational pathway assessments.

- Work with K–12 systems to align high school and college curriculum.

- Develop educational pathways/dual enrollment programs for high school students and onramp pathways for adults.

- Assist high school students and prospective adult students in obtaining financial aid and developing college success skills.

- Mandate new-student orientation and create opportunities for students to develop skills for college success.

- Provide early and continuous educational pathway advising, ensuring that all students enter a pathway as early as possible in their college experience. Initiate workforce readiness skill development and job placement advising early in the pathway experience.

Entry

- Redesign developmental education to reduce time to completion and expedite progress through educational pathways.

- Redesign the core curriculum, creating a core completion certificate.

- Engage students actively and effectively in all aspects of their college experience.

Progress

- Integrate advising into every student's ongoing educational experience.

- Incorporate hands-on learning through apprenticeships, internships, clinical placements, fieldwork, service learning, etc.

- Leverage technology to monitor student progress and intervene when appropriate with intrusive support.

- Celebrate student success milestones.

- Streamline automatic graduation when students meet requirements.

- Establish reverse transfer processes that apply university credits toward associate degrees that can be awarded after transfer.

- Align credentials with business and industry educational partners.

- Establish stackable credentials.

- Assure that degrees and certificates represent mastery of defined skills and competencies.

- Establish associate degree completion prior to transfer as the default plan for every student.

Completion

- Track student progress and success following university transfer.

Adapted from Completion by Design, an initiative funded by the Bill & Melinda Gates Foundation. http://completionbydesign.org/our-approach/our-model

Work Underway: Pathway Design and Implementation

- **Washington state's I-BEST (Integrated Basic Education and Skills Training)** program is a nationally recognized model through which a student rapidly increases his or her basic academic skills and/or English language proficiency while concurrently gaining workplace skills. This approach accelerates students' progress toward earning a credential and securing a living-wage job.

- At **Long Beach City College (CA)**, Promise Pathways—created in partnership with Long Beach Unified School District and California State University-Long Beach—builds a pathway from high school through university. At Long Beach City College, placement is based on high school achievement rather than test scores, and students develop first-semester success plans. Promise Pathways students sign a mutual responsibility agreement to participate, enroll full-time, complete key foundational courses beginning in their first semester, and participate in specific support activities such as a success course. Early results show significant increases in student completion of early educational milestones.

- The **Carnegie Foundation for the Advancement of Teaching** has involved 30 community colleges in eight states in early implementation of Statway, a mathematics pathway that leads students through developmental math to completion of a college-level statistics course in one academic year.

Statway features intensive student engagement, a strong focus on increasing student motivation and tenacity, and development of knowledge and skills needed for college navigation and academic success. Early results suggest that, compared to traditional approaches, Statway triples student success in half the time.

- **Stella and Charles Guttman Community College (NY)**, part of the City University of New York, established five degree pathways with specific learning sequences. The pathways permit only one or two electives during the entire degree program. Early data show student retention rates that far exceed those typically seen at other community colleges.

- **Miami Dade College (FL)** is a Completion by Design college where, to date, faculty have developed pathways in biology, business, criminal justice, and psychology—four of the college's five largest programs of study. Each of these associate degree pathways incorporates 36 general education credits and 24 credits in the program of study, all sequenced and designed to reinforce one another and to align students' work with upper-division courses. Developmental and English for Academic Purposes (EAP) onramp courses are aligned with gatekeeper courses (often in accelerated formats) to facilitate the transition to college-level study in math and English.

Dramatically improve college readiness

Dramatically improve college readiness: By 2020, reduce by half the numbers of students entering college unprepared for rigorous college-level work, and double the number of students who complete developmental education programs and progress to successful completion of related freshman-level courses.

A preponderant majority of community college students arrive at their college underprepared to succeed in college-level work. Finding ways to address this challenge far more effectively is essential if colleges are going to make progress in raising the numbers and rates of students completing college credentials.

Ⓐ Reducing the number of underprepared students entering college

How Can Colleges Do This Work?

Advice to colleges focuses on four actions:

- **Define and measure college readiness.** Use clear metrics and appropriate assessments to define college readiness, establish baseline data, and longitudinally track progress toward improved student outcomes.

- **Establish and support community partnerships.** Actively engage in collaborative work, such as pre-K through postsecondary and workforce (P–20W) consortia and other multisystem partnerships.

- **Participate in implementation of the Common Core State Standards (CCSS) or their equivalent in non-CCSS states.** Communicate with all involved stakeholders to ensure they are aware of the CCSS, the status of implementation, the cost to high school students and their families if students are not ready for college when they graduate, and the need to align career and college readiness skills. Partner with K–12 institutions to advocate for CCSS professional development.

- **Collaborate with K–12 partners.** Focus work in the 10 areas of engagement described at right.

COLLABORATING WITH K–12 PARTNERS

Improving students' success at college begins long before students enter college. Work with K–12 can include aligning curricula, early assessment and intervention, dual enrollment, and early college high schools.

AREA OF ENGAGEMENT	EXAMPLES
Create a college-going culture	Reach out to all levels of K–12 education through, for example, K–12/community college faculty summits. Expand early counseling on college options, financial aid, and opportunities to earn college credit while in high school.
Align expectations and curricula	Communicate specific expectations for college and career readiness to middle and high school counselors and students. Work with K–12 systems to create seamless pathways with aligned standards and curricula.
Support professional development	Align teacher preparation and development programs with the CCSS. Design cross-sector professional development opportunities for board members, faculty, and counselors.
Implement early interventions	Support early assessment (e.g., college placement assessments in sophomore or junior year of high school); support interventions (e.g., academic skill building and student success courses for high school students); and inform middle and high school faculty about college readiness predictors.
Expand dual/concurrent enrollment and early college high school programs	Promote strategies that enable students to earn college credit and even associate degrees while still in high school.
Evaluate program effectiveness	Assist K–12 educators in developing predictive models of persistence through K–12. Share methods for evaluating programs. Establish institutional research partnerships.
Refine program design and delivery	Organize K–12 and community college faculty discussions that link research and data to program design. Share new models and tools, such as competency-based credentials and learning analytics.
Strengthen uses of data to track success	Define and track metrics. Create data systems that facilitate longitudinal data analysis. Work with high schools to identify and track college readiness predictors.
Assess postsecondary readiness	Identify and assess predictors of postsecondary progress and success, using Voluntary Framework of Accountability metrics. Work with secondary schools to benchmark, evaluate, monitor, and share disaggregated data on college readiness.
Reimagine and reallocate resources	Assess the cost and efficacy of interventions to support data-informed allocation and reallocation of resources.

Work Underway: Increasing College Readiness

Define and measure college readiness

- Through its College Connections program, **Austin Community College (TX)** connects with Austin-area high school students to encourage them to attend college and help them successfully transition. The program provides free placement testing, assistance with college and financial aid applications, and college advising.

- The **Tennessee Higher Education Commission's** Seamless Alignment and Integrated Learning Support (SAILS) program helps high school students make sure they are prepared for college. The program includes a bridge math course that introduces a college's developmental math curriculum in the high school senior year.

Establish and support community partnerships

- **Florida's College Reach Out Program (CROP)** is a statewide initiative designed to strengthen college-going aspirations and preparation of low-income 8th- to 12th-grade students.

- The **West Virginia Department of Education** and the **West Virginia Community and Technical Colleges'** Earn a Degree, Graduate Early (EDGE) initiative promotes collaboration among high schools, colleges, and businesses. The tech-prep program offers a rigorous, seamless curriculum, work-based learning, and career development.

Participate in implementation of the Common Core State Standards

- Supported by a Core to College grant from a group of foundations, **Tillamook Bay Community College (OR)** and **Lane Community College (OR)** have worked with partner high schools and state universities to foster alignment of standards across sectors, based on the Common Core and related assessments.

Collaborate with K–12 partners

- When high school students take classes through **Greenfield Community College's (MA)** Educational Transitions program, they can earn college credit while completing requirements for high school graduation.

- **Maricopa Community Colleges' (AZ)** Achieving a College Education (ACE) program was created for high school students who either did not consider college or thought it was out of their reach. Students have the opportunity to take college courses in their junior and senior years of high school—and graduate from high school with up to 24 transferable college credits.

- **Gulf Coast Partners for Student Success (TX)** involves leaders, faculty, and staff from nine community colleges and 11 school districts in intensive work to align expectations and curricula, build a strong college-going culture, and ensure college readiness of high school graduates.

Where Can Colleges Learn More?

COMMON CORE STATE STANDARDS

- www.corestandards.org
- www.parcconline.org
- www.smarterbalanced.org

COLLEGE READINESS

- www.aascu.org/CollegeReadiness/ExecutiveSummary/
- www.ccrscenter.org

K–12/COMMUNITY COLLEGE COLLABORATION

- www.studentsuccessinitiatives.org/initiatives/current/gulf-coast-partners-achieving-student-success/

EARLY COLLEGE AND DUAL ENROLLMENT

- www.earlycolleges.org/Downloads/accelerated%20learning.pdf
- www.gatewaytocollege.org

B Doubling the number of students who complete developmental education programs and college-entry-level courses

How Can Colleges Do This Work?

Advice to colleges focuses on four areas of effective practice:

- **Strengthen pre-collegiate readiness and success.** This includes a set of actions that require close collaboration with K–12 systems, as described on page 15. Whether students come directly from high school or through other life experiences, community colleges then can propel students toward college readiness through summer bridge programs and/or intensive skill refreshers. Also promising are models integrating basic skills acquisition and workforce training, offered through partnerships involving colleges, workforce agencies, and service providers.

- **Provide college transitions support.** Key elements include mandatory and integrated placement test preparation, orientation, and advising; use of multiple measures (including high school transcripts and diagnostics) to inform mandatory placement; and elimination of late registration. Having students develop educational plans is essential, and as institutions design academic and career pathways, students should enroll in a defined program of study early in their college experience. Case management and intrusive advising ensure that students stay on track, as do high-tech/high-touch support services. Technologies and social media can support advising, registration, and academic alerts, while promoting interaction among students and with their instructors and advisors.

- **Redesign developmental education.** Community colleges have access to an increasing body of evidence about effective practice. Now colleges need to integrate more of these practices, at scale, into accelerated developmental pathways for all students who need them. Among the promising instructional models are combined/integrated courses, fast-track/flex courses, emporia, modularized curricula, and open-entry/open-exit approaches. All of these are enhanced by a student's continuous enrollment through completion of the developmental learning sequence. Learning communities, done well, can be highly effective.

Embedded academic and student supports are essential and may include co-requisite courses, supplemental instruction, and/or mandatory tutoring, along with intrusive advising. Also critical is integration of student success strategies—study skills, time management, tenacity, use of support services, financial literacy, and so on. Effective instructional approaches will emphasize engaged learning, integration of basic skills with academic or occupational content, and concrete applications of learning to work and life. Technology-enriched approaches include coordinated use of Khan Academy, flipped classrooms, and emporium models with embedded support.

- **Build the foundations for gateway course success.** Ultimately, the indicator of college readiness—and of effective developmental education—is successful completion of related college-level courses. Advisors can use multiple indicators of readiness (placement diagnostics, high school grades, etc.) to place students assessed at higher developmental levels into college-level courses with integrated co-requisites designed to provide additional support. Math pathways also show promise, because they integrate support while guiding student progress from developmental math to completion of college-level statistics or math. Technology-enabled supports and structured time on task, including supplemental instruction, have proven valuable.

Notably, every aspect of this work requires substantial commitments by colleges. They must commit to collaboration with K–12 partners; to professional development for full- and part-time faculty, advisors, and counselors; to bridging the divide between instruction and student services; to mending the disconnects between pre-college and college-level learning; to evidence-based teaching practice; and to creating multiple, intentional connections with and among students.

DESIGN PRINCIPLES FOR A DEVELOPMENTAL EDUCATION STUDENT SUCCESS PATHWAY

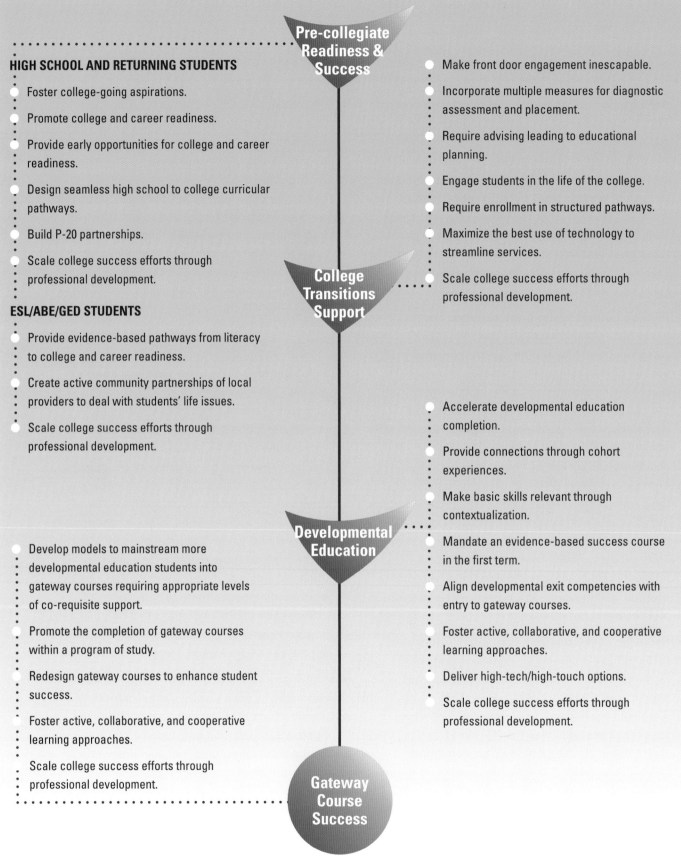

Pre-collegiate Readiness & Success

HIGH SCHOOL AND RETURNING STUDENTS

- Foster college-going aspirations.
- Promote college and career readiness.
- Provide early opportunities for college and career readiness.
- Design seamless high school to college curricular pathways.
- Build P-20 partnerships.
- Scale college success efforts through professional development.

ESL/ABE/GED STUDENTS

- Provide evidence-based pathways from literacy to college and career readiness.
- Create active community partnerships of local providers to deal with students' life issues.
- Scale college success efforts through professional development.

- Make front door engagement inescapable.
- Incorporate multiple measures for diagnostic assessment and placement.
- Require advising leading to educational planning.
- Engage students in the life of the college.
- Require enrollment in structured pathways.
- Maximize the best use of technology to streamline services.
- Scale college success efforts through professional development.

College Transitions Support

- Accelerate developmental education completion.
- Provide connections through cohort experiences.
- Make basic skills relevant through contextualization.

Developmental Education

- Develop models to mainstream more developmental education students into gateway courses requiring appropriate levels of co-requisite support.
- Promote the completion of gateway courses within a program of study.
- Redesign gateway courses to enhance student success.
- Foster active, collaborative, and cooperative learning approaches.
- Scale college success efforts through professional development.

- Mandate an evidence-based success course in the first term.
- Align developmental exit competencies with entry to gateway courses.
- Foster active, collaborative, and cooperative learning approaches.
- Deliver high-tech/high-touch options.
- Scale college success efforts through professional development.

Gateway Course Success

Work Underway: Redesigned Developmental Education

- **Community College of Baltimore County's (MD)** Accelerated Learning Program (ALP) invites students who place into upper-level developmental writing to become part of a 10-student cohort that takes English 101 concurrently with their developmental writing class. The two classes are taught by the same instructor and typically are scheduled during consecutive class periods. Independent research found that 74% of ALP students successfully completed English 101, as compared with 33% of students in the traditional developmental writing course. Moreover, 33% of the ALP students passed English 102, as compared with 10% of students in the traditional developmental course.

- The **Carnegie Foundation for the Advancement of Teaching's** collection of math pathways has two game-changing goals: (1) students will move through developmental education to earning credit in college-level math in one academic year; and (2) each student takes college math that is appropriate to his or her chosen program of study. Statway is a pathway that culminates with college-level statistics. About 50% of developmental math students entering Statway have earned college math credit in a year or less; by comparison, only 16% of traditional developmental math students in the same colleges earned college math credit in two years. Another pathway, Quantway, is focused on quantitative literacy and involves two courses: developmental math (Quantway 1) and college-level math (Quantway 2). About half of Quantway 1 students complete their developmental math requirements in a year. Sixty-eight percent of students entering Quantway 2 earn college-level math credit.

- The **New Mathways Project** involves all 50 Texas community college districts in statewide transformation of math education. The project, a joint effort of the **Charles A. Dana Center** at The University of Texas at Austin and the **Texas Association of Community Colleges,** aims to develop and fully implement three accelerated math pathways—statistics, quantitative literacy, and STEM—that will align with students' credential or career objectives. The pathways include intentional strategies to help students develop skills as learners.

- The **Virginia Community College System** has employed curriculum modularization as a key strategy for helping most students complete developmental math within one year. The developmental math curriculum has been redesigned into nine one-credit units. Students take only the modules they need, based on initial assessment and their own program of study. Mastery of content must be demonstrated before a student moves on to subsequent modules. Preliminary data show that within one year, 56% of students who took the new developmental mathematics placement test had either successfully completed their required developmental math units or were assessed as college-ready.

Where Can Colleges Learn More?

- Community College Research Center (CCRC) toolkit on developmental education redesign: http://ccrc.tc.columbia.edu/publications/designing-meaningful-developmental-reform.html

- Rutschow, E. Z., & E. Schneider (2011). *Unlocking the gate: What we know about improving developmental education.* New York, NY: MDRC.

- Information about Statway: www.carnegiefoundation.org/statway

- CCRC resources on accelerated developmental education: http://ccrc.tc.columbia.edu/research-project/accelerated-learning-program.html

- Resources from Student Success Initiatives at The University of Texas at Austin: www.studentsuccessinitiatives.org/resources/general-resources/pathway-to-student-success/

- Materials about the New Mathways Project from the Charles A. Dana Center: www.utdanacenter.org/higher-education/new-mathways-project/new-mathways-project-curricular-materials/

Close the American skills gap

Close the American skills gap by sharply focusing career and technical education on preparing students with the knowledge and skills required for existing and future jobs in regional and global economies.

To close the skills gap, community colleges will need to build capacity for identifying unfilled labor market needs and ensure that career education and training programs are targeted to address those high-need areas. They will also need to ensure students' opportunities for career advancement through the design of coherent career pathways leading to attainment of stackable credentials in those high-need areas. And they will need to build local, regional, and national partnerships (involving community colleges, employers, and government agencies) to accomplish a collaborative agenda that includes targeting skills gaps, promoting the associate degree as a desired employment credential, and establishing alternative models for completing skills-based credentials.

How Can Colleges Do This Work?

Advice to colleges focuses on four actions:

- **Better understand labor market trends and employers' needs—and communicate them to students.** Colleges should use current labor market information, such as projected jobs, employment trends, and wage data, to inform student advising. Student advising can include, for example, assessing students' interests and aptitudes, discussing relevant jobs, and exploring different educational pathways and the jobs/ salaries that would result from each. At the same time, colleges can strengthen employer engagement to learn about demand for skills

STACKABLE CREDENTIALS

Stackable credentials are a sequence of multilevel, industry-recognized credentials and/or certifications. They reflect mastery of the knowledge and skills required at different stages of a career or for multiple aspects of a profession. Stackable credentials include aligned entry and exit points, so students can earn credentials, work for some time, and then return to college for additional credentials without losing ground. This structure allows individuals to move along a career pathway, combining work with education to gain knowledge and skills—and advance to more senior (and higher paying) jobs.

Stackable credentials often are illustrated in terms of nursing because nursing education already is structured with a clear career pathway: a nursing assistant certificate, a licensed practical nurse (LPN) certificate, an associate degree in nursing (ADN) with a registered nurse (RN) license, a bachelor's degree in nursing (BSN), a master of science in nursing (MSN) or physician assistant (MPAS), and then the Ph.D.

Nursing: A Clear Path With Stackable Credentials

| 1 Nursing assistant certificate | 2 LPN | 3 ADN | 4 BSN | 5 MSN/MPAS | 6 Ph.D. |

in key local industries. With this information, colleges can project labor force needs as well as changes in the skill levels or composition of future jobs. Finally, colleges can engage industry subject matter experts to help develop in-depth competency-based curricula and credentials.

- **Develop career pathways for current and future jobs.** State policy, workforce development agencies, and community colleges should incorporate three intersecting elements: career pathway programs, sector strategies, and industry clusters. Community colleges can create pathways encompassing stackable, short-term programs that build toward more advanced credentials. They also can reduce learning time through assessments of prior learning, accelerated competency-based modules, and self-paced adaptive learning options. Then, colleges can provide pathways that incorporate a range of learning experiences—noncredit and industry-recognized programs, certifications, and credit programs and credentials—and lead students to employment and/or university transfer.

- **Redesign student experiences to incorporate more work-based, hands-on, and technology-enriched learning.** Effective educational practice will require more work-based learning, including internships, apprenticeships, and clinical placements. These programs are highly valued by employers and typically translate into workplace success. Colleges can increase use of simulators and trainers to improve hands-on competencies and bridge learning into the workplace. They also can incorporate open educational resources, including MOOCs and other technologies that facilitate access to learning and allow students to learn in both traditional classrooms and other settings.

- **Engage actively with partners to match education and training with jobs.** Closing skills gaps requires that community colleges deepen partnerships with business and industry to strengthen coordination, leverage resources, foster entrepreneurism, and support small business development. Close collaboration with Workforce Investment Boards and employers will help to build a pipeline for new workers in key sectors.

Work Underway: Closing the American Skills Gap

Better understand labor market trends and employers' needs

- **Walla Walla Community College (WA)** uses strong connections with local employers, sophisticated workforce data analysis, and extensive engagement in regional economic development to identify current and potential job growth. For example, the college played a central role in development of the region's vineyards and wineries by educating both the workers and the people who built the businesses. This effort helped the region update a slowing agriculture industry and replace jobs lost in other areas. The college also partners with the power company for program development in wind energy, another field with potential for job growth.

Develop career pathways for current and future jobs

- **Houston Community College (TX)** offers 11 entrepreneurship classes for those who seek to develop a business idea into a new business of their own and for those who want to expand their existing businesses. An eight-course sequence leads to a Certificate in Entrepreneurship.

Redesign student experiences to incorporate more work-based, hands-on, and technology-enriched learning

- **White Mountains Community College (NH)** is one of 11 institutions participating in a virtual incubator network. While many colleges have small-business incubators that help entrepreneurs through the challenges of starting a new business, the network shows that this support does not require a brick-and-mortar facility. Thus, it is a model for small, rural colleges that want to provide information and technical assistance to new businesses—and help increase jobs and revenue in their local communities.

- **Kentucky Community and Technical College System** is recognized as a pioneer in online education, providing options for students who cannot attend classes on campus due to scheduling conflicts, child care, work, or other commitments.

Engage actively with partners to match education and training with jobs

- To improve collaboration between community colleges and workforce leaders, **AACC** and the U.S. Conference of Mayors Workforce Development Council convened community college leaders and Workforce Investment Boards from across the country. The group discussed strategies for expanding effective collaborative models, joint advocacy, and strategic messaging.

- **William Rainey Harper College (IL)** has worked closely with 54 companies to create a program of stackable credentials that includes industry-endorsed certificates in manufacturing, paid internships, and pathways to associate and bachelor's degrees. Students are eligible for the paid internships when they earn the first-level certificate, which can be completed in less than four months. The college has received a $13 million federal grant to expand the program statewide.

Where Can Colleges Learn More?

- *A Guide for Using Labor Market Data to Improve Student Success:* www.aspeninstitute.org/sites/default/files/content/upload/AspenGuideforUsingLaborMarketData.pdf

- *The Role of Higher Education in Career Development: Employer Perceptions:* www.scribd.com/doc/128699977/The-Role-of-Higher-Education-in-Career-Development-Employer-Perceptions

Refocus the community college mission and redefine institutional roles

Refocus the community college mission and redefine institutional roles to meet 21st-century education and employment needs.

To ensure that students learn what they need to learn, community colleges should move toward a more open learning environment in which students can access services from a network of colleges, customize their learning, and choose from multiple modes of delivery. At the same time, institutions must explore new partnerships, staffing patterns, and business models, including consortium arrangements.

How Can Colleges Do This Work?

Advice to colleges focuses on six actions:

- **Develop the role of community colleges as brokers of educational opportunities rather than solely as direct providers of instruction.** Colleges can build a network of institutions and other service providers to meet students' varied educational needs. In this model, the individual community college sometimes provides services directly and sometimes directs students to alternative providers, much as Amazon serves its customers. One possibility, for example, is the creation of a college consortium with a shared curriculum so students can draw from the programs, courses, and delivery modes of every college in the network. A large regional network, or ultimately a national network, could

  have a universal catalog of defined competencies. Variations on that model include university centers that are coordinated by local community colleges and provide convenient access to upper-division and graduate education.

- **Strengthen the role of community colleges in advising, learning assessment, and credentialing.** Students are increasingly acquiring knowledge and skills in many settings and through many media over time. Thus, there is a growing need for expertise in helping students figure out how their individual learning adds up to credentials with value in the labor market. Developing community college strength in this role is timely, given increasing emphasis on competency-based learning. Evaluating each student's progress as she or he acquires knowledge and builds skills enhances individual and institutional productivity. It allows each student to focus on what he or she wants and needs to learn, and it minimizes time wasted on unnecessary work. And with competency-based learning, the value of credentials is clearly defined in terms of what students know and are able to do.

- **Redefine faculty roles.** Redesigned and more effective student experiences will require multiple dimensions of faculty expertise. Mastery of content will remain essential, but equally important will be expertise in effective teaching practices, curriculum pathway design, instructional technologies, learning assessment, student development, and so on. Colleges, therefore, must staff pathways with teams of educators that bring a great variety of talents and skills to the table. Making the most of each faculty member's knowledge and experience may require rethinking how faculty collaborate and define roles.

- **Create conditions in which part-time faculty can make their best contributions to student success.** In a sector where well over half of courses are taught by contingent faculty, colleges must rethink the ways they support these individuals so that they can fully contribute to the institution's effort to strengthen student learning and attainment.

- **Incorporate ingenious uses of technology in instruction and student services.** Technology companies and local institutions are developing useful tools to support individualized advising, academic planning, monitoring of student progress, learning assessment, early academic alert and intervention, and so on. Flipped classrooms and other technology-enriched approaches make the most of technological innovation while preserving the human connections that are critical to community college student success. Social media, texting, and creative uses of QR codes can promote students' connections to one another, to college faculty and staff, and to information about their studies and the support services available to them.

- **Empower students as partners in developing their paths and achieving their educational goals.** In the end, community colleges can advance the completion agenda only by intensively engaging students—in goal setting and choice of an academic/career pathway, in high-impact educational practices, and in purposeful interaction with other students, faculty, and advisors. Part of this engagement must include support for student development in critical areas, such as effort, tenacity, and skills for college success.

Work Underway: Refocusing Mission, Redefining Roles

Much of the reinvention called for in *Reclaiming the American Dream* and in this companion *Implementation Guide* still exists primarily in the aspirations of colleges and the imaginations of visionary leaders. Still, there are examples of work that point the way and illuminate possibilities for the future.

Develop the role of brokers of educational opportunities

- The **Global Corporate College** is a nationwide network of colleges that provides consistent, high-quality training for national and multinational corporations. For example, **Anne Arundel Community College (MD)** piloted TSA training for employees based at Baltimore/Washington International Thurgood Marshall Airport. The three-course pilot is part of the college's Homeland Security

Management associate degree program. The pilot was successful, and TSA scaled it up to provide training nationwide through the Global Corporate College.

- The **League for Innovation in the Community College** helps coordinate development of Homeland Security curricula, cataloging existing programs and promoting avenues for sharing across institutions.

- The **Lone Star College University Center (TX)** offers junior, senior, and graduate-level classes through partnerships with several universities. Students who enroll with one of the partner universities can complete a bachelor's or master's degree

ALIGNMENT OF LEARNING

Better alignment of learning is central to improving college completion. This includes alignment between high school graduation standards and college entry requirements, between community college exit competencies and university program requirements, and between the knowledge and skills gained in postsecondary education and those needed for current and emerging jobs in the labor market.

Competency-based learning—in which credits and credentials are based on mastery of skills and demonstrated expertise, rather than completion of courses—can be part of this alignment. Developing a competency-based learning model requires identifying specific skills and knowledge that students must master for each credential in each field.

In addition, community colleges must align learning within their own institutions, smoothing transitions between adult basic education, developmental education, and learning for college credit. Developing clear academic pathways will facilitate student progress from one level of credentialed learning to the next, and the next.

(or teaching certificate) without traveling to the university campuses.

- **Corporate College**, part of **Cuyahoga Community College (OH)**, provides training, organizational and professional development, event management, and other services for organizations and individuals, drawing from the resources of college faculty and programs as well as expertise across northeast Ohio.

- The **Auto Communities Consortium**, involving community colleges in **Illinois, Indiana, Iowa, Kentucky, Michigan, Ohio, Tennessee**, and **Wisconsin**, was organized to address common issues among communities where loss of hundreds of thousands of jobs has produced high unemployment rates. The network coordinates activities aimed at creating new jobs both within and outside the auto industry.

Strengthen advising, learning assessment, and credentialing

- Competency-based learning accommodates students who are learning new content, as well as those who bring prior learning from various sources. Relevant and intensive work is underway at **Western Governors University (WGU), Southern New Hampshire University**, and **Khan Academy**.

- The U.S. Department of Labor and the Bill & Melinda Gates Foundation have provided support for WGU to work with community colleges and employer partners to develop competency-based certificates and degrees, primarily in information technology fields. The work involves **Austin Community College (TX), Bellevue College (WA), Broward College (FL), Columbia Basin College (WA), Edmonds Community College (WA), Ivy Tech Community College (IN), Lone Star College System (TX), Sinclair Community College (OH), Spokane Falls Community College (WA)**, and **Valencia College (FL)**.

- **Lumina Foundation's** Tuning effort is a process to define, discipline by discipline, what knowledge and skills a student should master to earn an associate, bachelor's, or master's degree. Tuning can clarify expectations and facilitate transfer among institutions.

Redefine faculty roles

- At **Stella and Charles Guttman Community College (NY)**, every first-year student is a member of one of the college's houses (organizational structures that are much like learning communities). The college has no academic departments. Instead, a faculty instructional team leads each college house. The teams include faculty with discipline knowledge as well as expertise in other areas, a student success advocate, and CUNY graduate students who coordinate the students' studio experience (practice, reflection, and revision tied to classwork). A library staff member also attends all instructional team meetings.

Create conditions in which part-time faculty can make their best contributions

- Leading community colleges are working in a variety of ways to strengthen the role of part-time faculty. Profiles of approaches at **Bristol Community College (MA), Coastal Carolina Community College (NC), Community College of Vermont, County College of**

Morris (NJ), **Lake-Sumter State College (FL)**, **Richland College (TX)**, **Valencia College (FL)**, and **William Rainey Harper College (IL)** are included in a 2014 report from the Center for Community College Student Engagement, *Contingent Commitments: Bringing Part-Time Faculty Into Focus* (www.cccse.org).

Incorporate ingenious uses of technology in instruction and student services

- The **League for Innovation in the Community College, EDUCAUSE,** and the **Bill & Melinda Gates Foundation** are among the several partners in the Next Generation Learning Challenge initiative. **Montgomery County Community College (PA)** and **William Rainey Harper College (IL)** currently are involved in work to design breakthrough models for college completion. The **Kentucky Community and Technical College System, Rio Salado College (AZ),** and other institutions also have developed breakthrough models.

- My Academic Plan (MAP) is a technology-supported process for developing and monitoring each student's academic plan at **Sinclair Community College (OH).** Students work with an advisor to design an efficient program of study and then use the MAP system to view their plan and to find the classes needed to progress toward their goals. The MAP program links to the course catalog and to each student's schedule so they can always see where they are and what comes next. Sinclair has made the software available as open source, so a number of other colleges are adopting it.

- **St. Petersburg College (FL)** involved its faculty in developing the college's online early alert system. Faculty members use the system to notify staff about needed follow-up with students who are struggling academically. This system complements the online tool students use to develop an individualized learning plan, choose courses, and monitor their academic progress.

- **AACC** and **Khan Academy** are developing a partnership to support improvement in college readiness and developmental education outcomes.

Empower students as partners

- **Phi Theta Kappa,** the two-year college national honorary society, has empowered tens of thousands of community college students to commit to their own journey to graduation—and to bring fellow students and faculty with them—through the Community College Completion Corps (C4).

- The **PUENTE** project, implemented in numerous **California community colleges,** helps underserved students thrive academically by holding them to high expectations, honoring cultural and social capital, and giving students and their families critical information about college opportunities, choices, and success. Classes focus on multicultural and Latino literature. Students work with PUENTE counselors to set goals and develop educational plans.

- The **Center for Community College Student Engagement (CCCSE)** has surveyed more than 2.4 million community college students and conducted more than 200 student focus groups. *CCCSE* regularly reports findings to individual colleges and the community college field, thus helping ensure that student voices are heard as colleges seek to improve their educational experiences.

Where Can Colleges Learn More?

- Achieving the Dream is a national reform network focused on institutional transformation in support of student success and college completion. It provides a Knowledge Center and an Interventions Showcase: www.achievingthedream.org

- The League for Innovation in the Community College and EDUCAUSE are among the partners in the Next Generation Learning Challenge initiative: www.league.org/league/projects/nglc/ and www.educause.edu/ir/library/pdf/NG1233.pdf

- Christenson, C., Horn, M., Soares, L., & Caldera, L. (2011). *Disrupting college.* Washington, DC: Center for American Progress. www.americanprogress.org/wp-content/uploads/issues/2011/02/pdf/disrupting_college.pdf

- Oblinger, D. (2012). *Game changers: Education and information technologies.* Washington, DC: EDUCAUSE.

- Phi Theta Kappa's C4 campaign: www.cccompletioncorps.org

Invest in collaborative support structures

Invest in support structures to serve multiple community colleges through collaboration among institutions and with partners in philanthropy, government, and the private sector.

To increase institutional efficiency and strengthen service to students, groups of community colleges should pool resources and develop shared systems for managing student data, institutional research, professional development, and other efforts that support student learning.

How Can Colleges Do This Work?

Advice to colleges focuses on three actions:

- **Develop models for collaborative support structures and brokered/coordinated services.** Colleges can build alliances with other community colleges, universities, and community-based or national nonprofit organizations. The resulting partnerships can define shared goals, pool resources, and align operations and procedures.

- **Create statewide and border-crossing data systems.** These interactive systems ideally track students from pre-K through the K–12 system, community colleges, baccalaureate and graduate education, and into the workforce. They give colleges easy-to-access student data and tools to monitor student progress, institutional performance, and changes in community and labor force needs.

- **Create consortia to optimize the capacities of collaborating institutions.** Colleges—particularly small and rural institutions—can function with higher quality and lower cost through joint development of key resources, such as learning analytics technologies, institutional research operations, professional development programs, and purchasing cooperatives.

In addition, a national or regional network could develop and use a universal enterprise resource planning (ERP) system, which would offer cost savings, operational efficiencies, and the power of big data for analytics to the institutions and convenience and improved services for students.

Work Underway: Investments in Collaborative Support Structures

Collaborative support structures and brokered/coordinated services

- The campus library at **Ivy Tech Community College–Lafayette (IN)** is a joint effort between the college and the Tippecanoe County Public Library (TCPL). It serves both as a branch of the TCPL and as the main library for the college.

- The Black Mountain Campus, a partnership involving **Paradise Valley Community College (AZ)**, Desert Foothills YMCA, and the Foothills Community Foundation, is designed as a multigenerational neighborhood gathering place "for people of all ages to exercise both their minds and bodies." The campus provides education options, meeting spaces, and recreation facilities in one location.

- The **Virginia Community College System** has adopted a shared ERP system. The initiative allows for central processing of certain administrative functions and shared distance-learning courses.

- **Goodwill Industries** has launched more than 40 Goodwill-community college pilots, created in response to individual regions' identified skills needs. These programs reach out to lower-skilled, low-income adults, including the unemployed and underemployed, with a goal of increasing the number of financially stable households in the area. The programs encourage individuals to advance to successively higher levels of education and employment.

- The nonprofit **Single Stop USA** works with the **Association of Community College Trustees (ACCT)** and a growing number of colleges across the country to help low-income people achieve economic security. The one-stop program helps students assess their eligibility and apply for a variety of college supports. Single Stop has connected tens of thousands of community college students with well over $100 million in financial and other support, including tax credits, financial counseling, food stamps, and energy subsidies.

Statewide and border-crossing data systems

- Community and technical college systems in **Florida, Kentucky, North Carolina**, and **Washington** are often cited as examples of places where good work is underway in providing useful data on institutional performance and student progress.

- **Predictive Analytic Reporting (PAR) Framework**, a nonprofit, multi-institutional data mining collaborative, has 16 member institutions that share 1.7 million anonymous student records.

- At **Community Colleges of Spokane (WA)**, the collaborative Student Transitions Information Project bridges the educational data gap by combining K–12 records with data from the National Student Clearinghouse and the community colleges to create a longitudinal student data system for school districts and colleges in eastern and central Washington.

Create consortia

- The **Community College Consortium for Open Educational Resources**, originally established by the **Foothill–De Anza Community College District (CA)**, promotes development and use of open educational resources, open textbooks, and open courseware, both to expand access to higher education and to improve teaching and learning. Entities involved include individual community colleges, regional and statewide consortia, the Open Courseware Consortium, AACC, the League for Innovation in the Community College, and other educational partners.

Where Can Colleges Learn More?

- The Goodwill Industries program: www.aacc.nche.edu/Resources/aaccprograms/cwed/Pages/goodwill.aspx

- Washington Student Achievement Initiative: www.sbctc.ctc.edu/college/e_studentachievement.aspx

- Single Stop USA: www.singlestopusa.org

- The PAR Framework: www.wcet.wiche.edu/advance/par-framework

Target public and private investments strategically

Target public and private investments strategically to create new incentives for institutions of education and their students and to support community college efforts to reclaim the American Dream.

To make sure community college is affordable, colleges must make the most of every available funding stream—an effort that will require both ingenuity and advocacy at the local, state, and national levels. AACC collaborates with other policy information organizations to do this critical work, and colleges should contribute to the advocacy effort, both locally and at the state and national levels.

Policy is a critical tool for setting public priorities and strategically targeting public investments. As community colleges accelerate efforts to reclaim the American Dream, advocacy should focus on (1) generating renewed public and private investment in community colleges to support the public good; and (2) promoting policies that will both push and support community colleges in their work to improve college completion. At the same time, community colleges— particularly CEOs, with governing board support—must find innovative ways to diversify their revenue streams, while recognizing the very real challenge of managing resources in ways that achieve better outcomes at lower cost. This is the conundrum and the challenge of 21st-century leadership for community colleges.

How Can Colleges Partner With Others to Do This Work?

Success requires engaging in advocacy. On the state and federal levels, responsibility for advocacy is shared by AACC, the Association of Community College Trustees (ACCT), AACC councils and commissions, state systems and associations, and individual institutions. In addition to their participation through these entities, colleges can advocate directly through their state and federal representatives and their governors. This work depends on involvement of informed and active CEOs, trustees, faculty and staff, and student organizations, such as Phi Theta Kappa (PTK). For some colleges, these advocates may require training to develop skills in policy and advocacy. And for nearly all community college advocates, the next level of work will require the courage to promote public transparency and performance accountability, along with the flexibility to change traditional designs and funding for higher education.

In support of community college efforts to restore the middle class and reclaim the American Dream, community college advocates should support policies that advance the following objectives:

- **Ensure affordability.** Expanded funding for Pell Grants and restoration of the summer Pell are critical. Advocates also will push for reinstatement of the Pell Grant Ability to Benefit option to allow students without a high school diploma or a high school equivalency credential to participate in higher education.

- **Promote college completion.** New public funding models that promote and reward college completion will better serve colleges and their students. Innovative funding models should include incentives for colleges to preserve access and continue serving high-risk and traditionally underserved students. Updated financial aid programs can include incentives for students to focus on their own progress and achievement. And new, evidence-based policies can support colleges in reducing the need for developmental education while dramatically increasing completion of both developmental education and related college-level courses. Policy also can promote innovation and efficiency through non-course-based funding.

- **Strengthen transparency and accountability.** Policy leaders at the local, state, and federal levels should recognize the Voluntary Framework of Accountability (VFA) as a set of accepted metrics for community college performance and improvement. Colleges will be more transparent and consistent—and their data burden will be reduced—if federal policy designates the National Student Clearinghouse as the official provider of accountability data for the VFA and all federal metrics. Perhaps most important is public investment in data systems that can be used to track students' progress—within individual institutions and education sectors, through transitions from one education sector to the next, and into the workforce.

- **Build seamless transitions across education sectors.** Local governing boards, as well as state and federal policymakers, should provide incentives for comprehensive P–20 partnerships. These incentives can encourage institutions to work across education sectors to give students clear pathways to further education and careers. State policy also can require actions that fix the community college/university transfer process, including measures to reduce students' loss of credits, ensure quality by basing credits on students' demonstrated mastery of specified knowledge and skills, and provide incentives for students to complete associate degrees before transferring.

- **Connect education and jobs.** State officials should take steps to officially designate community colleges as the state's primary providers of workforce education and training. At the federal level, continued funding of Trade Adjustment Assistance Community College and Career Training (TAACCCT) grants will enable community colleges to provide programs needed to meet the needs of employers and to support economic growth. At all levels, advocates should pursue discussions about augmented funding for job training, particularly for the long-term unemployed.

Work Underway: Strategically Targeting Public Investments

Ensure affordability

- Proposals have been offered in **Tennessee** and **Oregon** to consider making community college education free, at least for a stipulated period of enrollment time and with satisfactory academic performance.

- Through **Benefits Access for College Completion,** seven community colleges are working to fill the gap between financial aid and the resources needed to attend and persist in college. The colleges are testing ways to connect students to supports including childcare subsidies, food assistance, and tax credits. The work is funded by a collaborating group of foundations and managed by the **Center for Law and Social Policy** and **AACC.** Participants in the implementation phase are **Cuyahoga Community College (OH), Gateway Community and Technical College (KY), LaGuardia Community College (NY), Lake Michigan College (MI), Macomb Community College (MI), Northampton Community College (PA),** and **Skyline College (CA).**

Promote college completion

- According to a recent report from the National Center for Higher Education Management Systems (NCHEMS) and Complete College America, more than a quarter of states are currently implementing outcomes-based funding in at least one higher education sector, and numerous other states are moving in that direction.

- In **Tennessee,** 100% of state higher education funding is based on performance measures including student retention, degrees earned, and developmental courses completed. Institutions also can earn rewards based on the number of students who complete 24, 48, or 72 credits.

- Community college presidents in **Ohio** began 2014 with a bold new proposal to move further from enrollment-based funding to outcomes-based funding. State dollars would be allocated to community colleges based on students' completion of credentials or transfer to a baccalaureate institution.

- In 2009, the **Texas** legislature adopted a new developmental education policy: Include non-course-based developmental education interventions—for example, intensive skills brush-up programs—in the state's community college formula-funding system. Colleges file reports with the state agency on non-course-based interventions, which are included as part of the funding request to the Texas legislature.

Strengthen transparency and accountability

- With support from the Lumina Foundation, **Arizona's 10 independent community college districts** collaborated to develop a national model for

---

Where Can Colleges Learn More?

- Collins, M. L. (2009). *Setting up success in developmental education: How state policy can help community colleges improve success.* Boston, MA: Jobs for the Future.

- Complete College America. (2013). *The game changers: Are states implementing the best reforms to get more college graduates?* www.completecollege.org/pdfs/CCA%20Nat%20Report%20Oct18-FINAL-singles.pdf

- Jones, D. (2013). *Outcomes-based funding: The wave of implementation.* Washington, DC: Complete College America. www.completecollege.org/pdfs/Outcomes-Based-Funding-Report-Final.pdf

- President Barack Obama announced a White House plan to make college more affordable for American families: www.whitehouse.gov/the-press-office/2013/08/22/fact-sheet-president-s-plan-make-college-more-affordable-better-bargain-

- Jobs for the Future addresses funding: http://knowledgecenter.completionbydesign.org/sites/default/files/367%20JFF%20Altstadt%202012.pdf

performance-based funding. The model was inspired by the 2011 *Arizona Community Colleges: Long-Term Strategic Vision,* which defined indicators of progress toward goals of access, retention, and completion. Many of the metrics are aligned with those included in the VFA, which will allow for comparisons with national norms in the future. The state has undertaken a pilot of the first phase of the performance funding model.

- See pages 35–36 for additional examples of strengthening transparency and accountability.

Build seamless transitions across education sectors

- The state of **Maryland's** College and Career Readiness and College Completion Act of 2013 illustrates a visible effort to reimagine systems and reallocate resources. Its requirements include assessing college readiness no later than 11th grade, a single statewide transfer agreement, and a single statewide reverse transfer agreement.

- In **California,** the Student Transfer Achievement Reform Act (SB 1440) guarantees that community college students who complete an associate degree designated for transfer will be admitted to the California State University system with

junior status. It further ensures they will be given priority consideration for admission to their local California State University campus and to a particular program that is similar to the student's community college major.

- The **Louisiana** Transfer Degree Guarantee, established through state legislation, helps students easily transfer from a community college to a public four-year university in Louisiana. The Transfer Degree Guarantee ensures that a community college student, upon completion of a 60-hour general education block, can transfer to a Louisiana four-year public university and enroll with junior-level status in the college or university.

Connect education and jobs

- In 2003, the state of New Jersey designated community colleges as the primary providers of workforce training in the state. The Center for Business & Technology at **College of Morris (NJ),** for example, works with businesses to provide customized employee education. The college assesses employees' training needs and provides flexible scheduling, hands-on instruction, and classes at the work site or on campus.

Implement policies and practices that promote rigor and accountability

Implement policies and practices that promote rigor, transparency, and accountability for results in community colleges.

To promote rigor and accountability, community colleges nationwide should implement the Voluntary Framework of Accountability (VFA) and improve measurement of student learning and employment-related outcomes.

At the same time, states should implement statewide data systems so colleges can track students on their educational and career pathways. Statewide data systems also will help education leaders demonstrate the employment- and wage-related results of a community college education.

TRANSPARENCY AND ACCOUNTABILITY: THE VFA

The VFA is the first national system of accountability for community colleges. Developed by AACC, ACCT, and the College Board with broad institutional involvement, the VFA gauges the performance of community colleges in terms of their unique mission and their diverse students. Before the VFA, community colleges were largely assessed using measures developed for baccalaureate institutions, so the assessment was not well aligned with community college work. For example, measures often were pegged to full-time students, who represent less than half of the community college student population.

How Can Colleges Do This Work?

Advice to colleges focuses on two actions:

- **Implement the VFA.** Indicate publicly the college's commitment to and implementation of the VFA.

- **Develop and use common indicators of student success.** Work with states, funders, and national associations to develop a concise set of consistently defined indicators of student progress and success.

At the same time, to build and strengthen the college-level work, the following actions should happen at the national level:

- **Develop the VFA's workforce metrics to incorporate labor and wage data that reflect outcomes of community college education.** This work should include developing standard data definitions and collection methods so data can be useful nationally and incorporated into state systems.

- **Continue work to strengthen ways of reporting student learning outcomes as part of the VFA.** It is important to colleges and the public to ensure that increased numbers of postsecondary credentials represent high-quality learning outcomes.

- **Encourage colleges nationwide to adopt the VFA, and promote statewide participation.** By 2015, at least 50% of community colleges should adopt the VFA and/or colleges using the framework should account for at least 50% of community college enrollments. By 2018, 80% of AACC member colleges should adopt the VFA. By 2020, 100% of AACC member colleges should be using the tool.

- **Position the VFA as the standard for measuring community college performance.** For example, work with the U.S. Department of Education to incorporate the VFA in the reauthorization of the Higher Education Act; encourage entities including the U.S. Department of Education's Integrated Postsecondary Education Data System (IPEDS), Achieving the Dream, and the Aspen Prize for Community College Excellence to use the VFA metrics in their data collection and evaluations; and advocate use of the VFA to drive state performance funding and the design of state data systems.

- **Support colleges so they can use the VFA effectively.** Build connections with the Council for the Study of Community Colleges, Association for Institutional Research, and other research organizations, and develop a technical support network for colleges with smaller institutional research offices.

- **Establish an annual evaluation of the VFA's effectiveness.** This assessment should address the percentage of colleges that have adopted the framework, the alignment of the VFA with other tools, user satisfaction, and website analytics.

Work Underway: Promoting Rigor and Accountability

Using the VFA

- **Oxnard College (CA)** uses VFA data to identify and remove roadblocks to progression and credential completion. For example, VFA data led the college to invest in improving tutoring labs.

- **Maricopa Community College (AZ)** and **Cochise Community College (AZ)** were the first two Arizona colleges to do a thorough examination of the VFA measures. Arizona adopted the measures that worked for its colleges and introduced the framework to the Arizona Community College Association. At the association level, the presidents recommended use of selected VFA metrics in the state's performance accountability model.

- Through the **Pennsylvania Commission on Community Colleges,** all 14 Pennsylvania community colleges agreed to adopt the VFA statewide, with **Montgomery County Community College (PA)** as a lead advocate. The colleges use the VFA to improve pedagogy, to benchmark performance relative to one another, and to collectively examine and present state-level outcomes for their students.

- Several states, including **Iowa, Michigan,** and **New York,** are exploring the use of VFA data to set on-campus performance indicators, streamline reporting formats, and possibly collect data at the state level.

Extending and strengthening the VFA

- The **Student Achievement Measure (SAM),** which incorporates selected VFA metrics, improves reporting of student progress and graduation by including a greater proportion of an institution's undergraduate students as well as tracking students who enroll in multiple higher education institutions. Typical measures of student progress and completion, including government-led efforts, usually underreport student achievement because they do not account for an increasingly mobile student population. SAM is a joint initiative of the six national higher education presidential associations: the **AACC,** the **American Association of State Colleges and Universities (AASCU),** the **American Council on Education (ACE),** the **Association of American Universities (AAU),** the **Association of Public and Land-grant Universities (APLU),** and the **National Association of Independent Colleges and Universities (NAICU).**

- The **Degree Qualifications Profile (DQP)** provides a framework for assessing student learning outcomes at the associate degree level and thus offers the potential of incorporating student learning into the VFA. The framework clearly states what students should be expected to know and be able to do once they earn a degree, regardless of a student's field of specialization. In **Oregon,** all seven Oregon University System (OUS) institutions and the state's 17 independent community colleges are developing Oregon's DQP, which will describe institutions' degree outcomes across the state.

- **AACC, AASCU,** and **APLU** have proposed a collaborative effort to assemble and report postcollegiate outcomes so colleges can use the data to improve. The effort would define postcollegiate outcomes metrics and recommend actions to improve colleges' ability to access, report, and analyze workforce outcomes.

Where Can Colleges Learn More?

- VFA brochure: http://vfa.aacc.nche.edu/Documents/VFABrochureLowResolution.pdf
- VFA toolkit: http://vfa.aacc.nche.edu/marketing/Pages/default.aspx
- www.dqpp.org/associates-degree
- www.luminafoundation.org/publications/The_Degree_Qualifications_Profile.pdf

Leading and Working Differently

Implementing change is about working differently. Shepherding many of the strategies described in this *Implementation Guide*—including pathways, stackable credentials, and competency-based learning—will require significant resources and political capital.

Colleges, therefore, will have to restructure priorities and reallocate resources to accomplish the critical work called for in *Reclaiming the American Dream*. To do so, colleges will need to attend to two essentials: leadership and faculty engagement.

How Can Colleges Do This Work?

Leadership

College CEOs should commit to the following:

- Invest in leadership development of their senior and mid-level administrators, as well as their faculty and staff. Develop the pipeline of future community college leaders who embrace and exhibit the *AACC Competencies for Community College Leaders.*

- Make the CEO accountable for student success outcomes, particularly college completion and equity.

- Align hiring and evaluation processes with advancing the institution's student success agenda.

- Ensure that the student success agenda is a prime driver for operating and capital budgets.

Governing boards should commit to the following:

- Establish and participate in trustee leadership development, particularly emphasizing policy governance in support of student success and college completion.

- Embrace the competencies outlined in *AACC Competencies for Community College Leaders* in defining CEO expectations, particularly with regard to risk-taking and change management.

- Invest in continuing leadership development of the CEO as integral to sustaining and advancing the institution's long-term strategic goals.

- Adopt and support accountability measures, such as the VFA, to advance completion of degrees or certificates that lead to a living wage.

Faculty Engagement

To develop and encourage faculty leadership for student success, colleges should engage faculty as leaders in the following work:

- Establish a broad demand for change by demonstrating that the status quo is not sufficient, citing data to build a sense of urgency for reform.

- Engage faculty colleagues (including part-time faculty) in open and frank discussions about why improving learning outcomes, student success, and certificate/degree completion matters to the college, community, state, and nation.

- Identify and draw on each faculty member's strengths and expertise, particularly in areas not specifically limited to their discipline (e.g., developing curriculum, assessing learning, and using learning technologies).

- Redesign pedagogy and course content to meet the needs, learning styles, and expectations of 21st-century students.

- Encourage faculty to take ownership in the design of professional development programs and other experiences that lead to improved learning outcomes and success for a student population that is increasingly diverse in terms of race and ethnicity, learning styles, level of academic preparedness, and life experiences.

- Diversify the faculty so it more adequately reflects the student population.

- Ensure that full-time and part-time faculty work together to strengthen learning outcomes and student success. Provide part-time faculty with full-time faculty mentors. Provide a certification program through which part-time faculty can practice effective teaching methods, learn about active learning strategies, and increase knowledge about the campus, student support systems, and college policies.

- Assume responsibility for involving part-time faculty in developing and implementing a student success agenda.

State and National Strategies

- Encourage state faculty associations to provide professional development opportunities focused on the design and adoption of innovative instruction that meets the needs of 21st-century college students.

- Engage national education associations in discussions about the changing roles and responsibilities of faculty in the nation's 21st-century colleges.

- Encourage state and national faculty unions to establish professional development programs and experiences and provide resources that encourage, recognize, and reward use of evidence-based, high-impact educational practices.

Work Underway: Leadership and Faculty Engagement

- **Achieving the Dream (ATD)** emphasizes the importance of transformational leadership and broad faculty engagement in the student success agenda through its work with colleges in the ATD network, its publications, and its annual DREAM Institute on Student Success.

- **Community College of Vermont** emphasizes professional development for its all-part-time faculty; **Sinclair Community College (OH)** and **Richland College (TX)**, among others, have developed robust professional development programs for part-time faculty members.

- The acclaimed learning communities work at **Kingsborough Community College (NY)** is a faculty-led transformation that has led to improvements in student success.

- At **Tallahassee Community College (FL)**, faculty engagement is key to the success of the Learning Commons, a specially designed space that centralizes learning and technology support for all students. Faculty members can schedule office hours there, and collaboration between faculty and staff helps students with academics, learning strategies, and technology skills. This transformation in ways of working has resulted in substantially increased numbers of students using and benefiting from academic support.

The **League for Innovation in the Community College** established the John & Suanne Roueche Excellence Awards to recognize and celebrate outstanding contributions and leadership by community college faculty and staff. Recipients are honored during the League's annual Innovations conference.

Where Can Colleges Learn More?

- The Aspen Institute is an educational and policy studies organization. The Institute provides leadership and policy programs, produces a number of publications, and hosts issue-focused seminars and meetings: www.aspeninstitute.org

- www.aacc.nche.edu/newsevents/Events/leadershipsuite/ Pages/competencies.aspx

FOR CEOS

- Executive Leadership Institute, conducted by the League for Innovation in the Community College: www.league.org/eli/

- Future Presidents Institute, sponsored by AACC: www. aacc.nche.edu/newsevents/Events/leadershipsuite/Pages/ fliadvanced.aspx

- Harvard Seminar for New Presidents, sponsored by the Harvard Graduate School of Education: www.gse.harvard. edu/ppe/programs/higher-education/portfolio/new-presidents.html

- Leadership Symposium and Leadership Fellows Program, offered by the National Community College Hispanic Council, an AACC affiliate: www.ncchc.com

- The Thomas Lakin Institute for Mentored Leadership, sponsored by the Presidents' Round Table, National Council on Black American Affairs, an AACC affiliate: http://theprt. pgcc.edu/LakinInstitute.aspx

- The Leaders Institute, sponsored by the American Association of Women in Community Colleges: www. aawccnatl.org/leaders-institute

FOR BOARDS OF TRUSTEES

- Governance Institute for Student Success, a model that blends the Governance Leadership Institute of the Association of Community College Trustees (ACCT) and the Board of Trustees Institute developed by Student Success Initiatives at the University of Texas: www.governance-institute.org

- New and Experienced Trustees Governance Leadership Institute, ACCT: www.acct.org/events/institute/

The Next Big Things

The 21st-Century Initiative calls for unprecedented transformation in community colleges across the country. Change at this scope requires collaborative efforts and a strong sense of urgency, coupled with long-term commitments to work that is intellectually and politically complex.

This *Implementation Guide* gives colleges ideas, examples, and resources to support early and important steps. However, not all of the work can be quickly accomplished, nor effectively undertaken by community colleges alone. In fact, certain large-scale, substantive changes will require a concerted national effort to address critical systemic and policy issues.

Therefore, the implementation teams and their Steering Committee are recommending a limited set of action priorities that will help guide AACC's national leadership for community colleges over the next three to five years: These are **The Next Big Things.** They include: leading an intensified commitment to college completion, strengthening accountability, supporting work to design and implement student pathways, hosting a national working summit on college readiness and developmental education redesign, creating a seamless education and career system, and building stackable credentials and a national credentialing system.

These tasks are big, urgent, and therefore expensive. They certainly will require extensive collaboration across education sectors, philanthropy, federal and state agencies, and the national community college/higher education organizations.

But they also are worth the investment of these dollars and hours because they are the key to transforming colleges so they better serve students and the nation. Following are brief descriptions of these next big things for community colleges.

Leading an Intensified Commitment to College Completion

Short-term strategies—the low-hanging fruit for college efforts to increase completion—will include the following, implemented at greatly increased scale:

- Automatic awards of credentials to students who have earned them.

- Reverse transfer arrangements with universities and other community colleges.

- Programs to bring back students who need only a limited number of additional credits to complete a credential.

In addition, it will be important to conduct strategic communication campaigns that impress upon students (as well as their families and college faculty and staff) the importance of college completion. The potential impact of such campaigns is illustrated by Phi Theta Kappa's (PTK) intensive focus on the Community College Completion Corps (C4).

Longer-term strategies will include the following:

- Using new and emerging technologies to strengthen advising, academic planning, and monitoring processes.

- Better aligning curriculum across levels of learning, from high school or GED/ABE through developmental education, college-level work in the community college, and university coursework.

- Statutory and regulatory changes that ensure transferability of credits earned in an agreed-upon curriculum, for application to the major program in transfer institutions.

- Policy changes at the state and local levels that encourage full-time college attendance when feasible for students, incorporate completion incentives in financial aid programs, reward colleges through new funding mechanisms for improving their completion rates while preserving access, and strengthen capabilities for tracking student progress through educational levels, through multiple institutions, and into the workforce.

Strengthening Community College Accountability

National organizations for community colleges, led by AACC and with the support of numerous local colleges, have come together to design, test, and refine the Voluntary Framework of Accountability (VFA). This accountability framework is appropriate to the missions and student populations served by community colleges.

The increasing level of institutional participation is now fueled by a number of commitments to statewide participation. To realize fully the potential of the VFA— seen in transparency, accountability, the benefits of benchmarking, and the promise of improved performance—the community college field must fully participate in submitting and using the data.

To **broaden VFA participation and impact,** AACC and others will work to implement the following:

- Information sessions for college governing boards, followed by their formal commitments to participation in the VFA.

- Significant changes in data reported to IPEDS, incorporating and/or modifying data elements to make them consistent with the VFA—and thus also reducing reporting burdens for institutions.

- Promotion of further state-level adoption of the VFA as a whole or of particular performance metrics defined for the VFA.

In addition to a major effort to engage the community college field far more extensively in the VFA, the field needs continued efforts to **augment and refine the performance indicators.** To ensure appropriate reporting on key missions of community colleges, priority should be given to these next-level tasks:

- Development of standard metrics that will serve as indicators of the performance of community colleges in workforce preparation.

- Continuing work to incorporate appropriate indicators of student learning outcomes into the accountability framework.

Given the many entities now joining in calls for improved performance of higher education institutions and dramatically increased college completion rates, it is essential to have a concerted effort to **align a core set of performance metrics across multiple initiatives, agencies, and geographic lines.** Identifying a limited number of key performance indicators for community colleges will require the collaboration of national community college organizations, philanthropic foundations, and government agencies at the state and federal levels.

Supporting Work to Design and Implement Pathways

Colleges must design new educational pathways that will provide increased clarity, structure, and coherence. The pathways should lead to significantly increased completion of certificates and degrees that prepare students for family-supporting careers. There is no single blueprint for this work; but there is emerging consensus on a set of design principles that are supported by evidence. Even more important, there are colleges leading the way by actually doing this work.

To expand that bold work, the national community college leadership organizations and other partners, supported by AACC, can provide a series of regional pathway design institutes for college leadership teams across the country. These institutes would build on foundation-funded initiatives and local efforts. AACC also can provide pertinent research, examples, and other information resources to support the work through its 21st-Century Center (www.aacc21stcenturycenter.org).

Hosting a National Working Summit on College Readiness and Developmental Education Redesign

College readiness efforts are an essential part of developing on-ramps to pathways—and of educating low-income and underserved populations. Thus, if community colleges are to achieve their ambitious goals for increased college completion, the inevitable and central imperative is to address twin challenges: substantially improved college readiness of students entering the institutions, and dramatically improved effectiveness of developmental education for the large numbers of students who will continue to need it.

The goals established in *Reclaiming the American Dream* call on institutions to demonstrate these outcomes by 2020:

- Reduce by half the number of students entering college unprepared for rigorous college-level work.

- Double the number of students who complete developmental education programs and progress to successful completion of related freshman-level work.

Over the past decade, a great deal has been learned about what needs to be done to achieve these goals. In fact, more is known than is currently being implemented at scale on campuses across the country. As highlighted through the 21st-Century Initiative, the community college field now has access both to emerging evidence and to telling examples of colleges where results are improving substantially.

To broaden the implementation of key design principles and evidence-based practices in strengthening college readiness and developmental education, AACC will engage partner organizations and national experts in hosting a national working summit to facilitate the necessary redesign efforts. The work of the summit will be guided by data and informed by evidence.

The first half of the summit will bring community college leadership teams together with leaders from their K–12 partner districts to develop concrete action plans for collaborative work to align high school graduation requirements with college readiness standards, build a college-going culture, increase college credits earned by high school students, provide appropriate college success courses for high school students, work with prospective college students and their families on college admission and financial aid applications, and so on. Designing academic and career pathways that students can follow from high school through to completion of community college and university credentials will be crucial long-term work.

In the second half of the summit, community college leadership teams will develop plans to make their institutions more effective in developmental education—so more students complete both developmental education and college-level courses. The summit will emphasize strategies for acceleration of student progress, curriculum changes such as modularization and contextualization, using pathways rather than course sequences, and uses of technology that strike the balance between capitalizing on innovative potential and ensuring the human connections that are critical to community college student success.

Creating a Seamless Education and Career System

For years, or even decades, educators and policymakers have called repeatedly for action to ensure that students can readily progress across sector boundaries without losing momentum, credit, or time. Yet those losses continue to characterize the educational experiences of far too many students, exacting costs to them as individuals as well as to taxpayers and the society.

Full implementation of the 21st-Century Commission's recommendations rests on the effort of local and state education and policy leaders to *mind the gaps*. The work entails aligning standards and curriculum within and across education systems. It also requires assessment systems that not only connect with those standards but also award credit for prior learning. Moreover, as noted above, it depends on regulatory and statutory measures that ensure transferability of students' earned credits across postsecondary institutions.

In addition to the work within education, there is an urgent call to close the skills gaps—the troublesome discrepancies between the skills needed in the American workforce and the skills possessed by graduates of America's educational institutions. Creating the seamless transition between education and work requires another level of collaboration—in this case, among postsecondary education, employers, and their respective agencies and organizations—so that colleges are offering the programs and teaching the knowledge and skills that will effectively prepare students for a rapidly changing and globally competitive labor market.

Addressing this issue requires an aggressive and coherent national strategy, appropriately led by AACC and matched with complementary and essential work at the state, regional, and local levels. The design of this multiple-level policy and practice strategy will become a key priority for AACC over the next three years.

Building Stackable Credentials and a National Credentialing System

Competency-based education is hardly a new concept. But with today's multiple education providers and platforms, colleges have a new imperative to clearly define what students should know and be able to do as a result of their educational experiences—and to effectively assess students' knowledge and skills.

Beyond the definition of competencies is the accelerated development of stackable credentials—a coherent system of increasingly advanced and carefully aligned learning in specific fields of study that allows and encourages Americans to augment their learning, and thus their career advancement and earning power, over time. Clarity about requisite knowledge and skills at each level of learning must be complemented with common systems for documenting student competencies, providing credentials with portability for students, and assuring quality for education providers.

This is no simplistic or reductionist endeavor; rather, it is intellectually, politically, and logistically demanding.

AACC, in collaboration with colleges, states, multiple government agencies, and industry partners, is perfectly positioned to lead a major strategic effort.

Ultimately, community colleges and their organizational partners, including universities, K–12 education, philanthropy, and state and federal agencies, seek to **develop and implement a national credentialing system.** Implementation of such a system should include guidelines for working with new micro-credentialing tools such as digital badges and e-portfolios. A well-designed system would support documentation of students' acquired competencies, ensure currency and quality in education and training, and promote achievement of national, state, and individual goals for increased educational attainment and sustained economic competitiveness.

Imagine Success

To reclaim the American Dream, community colleges are called to reimagine their institutional missions and roles for the 21st century and to redesign their students' experiences to ensure that millions more Americans realize that dream. The work outlined in this *Implementation Guide* is extensive but also exciting, daunting but also doable. In the end, it also is simply necessary.

To undertake this work, colleges will collaborate with others, conduct courageous conversations, and examine data. They also must bring students into the conversation—ask their opinions, hear their voices, and take note of their ideas. Just as students and colleges are partners in learning, they can and should be partners in improving the college experience—both for themselves and for those who will follow.

Lighting the way through the challenges—constrained resources, complex politics, community college people and partners working harder than perhaps they ever thought they could—there is the vision of success: a nation with a restored middle class, with a growing edge toward equity, with a democracy and an economy that works for everyone.

Empowering Community Colleges to Build the Nation's Future

AACC 21st-Century Initiative
Steering Committee and Implementation Teams

Walter G. Bumphus, President & CEO, American Association of Community Colleges (DC)

Steering Committee

Co-Chairs

Rey Garcia, President & CEO, Texas Association of Community Colleges (TX)

Alex Johnson, President, Cuyahoga Community College (OH)

Steven Lee Johnson, President, Sinclair Community College (OH)

E. Ann McGee, President, Seminole State College of Florida (FL)

Karen A. Stout, President, Montgomery County Community College (PA)

Members

J. David Armstrong, Jr., President, Broward College (FL)

Ken Atwater, President, Hillsborough Community College (FL)

Helen Benjamin, Chancellor, Contra Costa Community College District (CA)

Cynthia A. Bioteau, District President, Florida State College at Jacksonville (FL)

J. Noah Brown, President & CEO, Association of Community College Trustees (DC)

Richard Carpenter, Chancellor, Lone Star College System (TX)

Gerardo E. de los Santos, President & CEO, League for Innovation in the Community College (AZ)

Myrtle E. B. Dorsey, Chancellor, St. Louis Community College District (MO)

Kevin E. Drumm, President, SUNY Broome Community College (NY)

Charlene M. Dukes, President, Prince George's Community College (MD)

Johanna Duncan-Poitier, Sr. Vice Chancellor for Community Colleges and the Education Pipeline, The State University of New York (NY)

Kenneth L. Ender, President, William Rainey Harper College (IL)

Katharine Eneguess, President, White Mountains Community College (NH)

Rufus Glasper, Chancellor, Maricopa County Community College District (AZ)

Marie Foster Gnage, President, West Virginia University at Parkersburg (WV)

Gregory J. Hamann, President, Linn-Benton Community College (OR)

Brenda Hellyer, Chancellor, San Jacinto College District (TX)

James Jacobs, President, Macomb Community College (MI)

Jane A. Karas, President, Flathead Valley Community College (MT)

Brent Knight, President, Lansing Community College (MI)

Scott Lay, President & CEO, Community College League of California (CA)

Michael B. McCall, President, Kentucky Community and Technical College System (KY)

Shaun L. McKay, President, Suffolk County Community College (NY)

Cindy L. Miles, Chancellor, Grossmont–Cuyamaca Community College District (CA)

Daniel J. Phelan, President, Jackson College (MI)

Camille Preus, President, Blue Mountain Community College (OR)

R. Scott Ralls, President, North Carolina Community College System (NC)

Rod A. Risley, Executive Director, Phi Theta Kappa (MS)

Sanford C. "Sandy" Shugart, President, Valencia College (FL)

Jennifer Wimbish, President, Cedar Valley College (TX)

P. Anthony Zeiss, President, Central Piedmont Community College (NC)

AACC Staff Liaison

Sarah Cale-Henson, Program Manager, 21st-Century Initiative

Implementation Team 1: Community College Completion Commitment

Co-Chairs

J. Noah Brown, President & CEO, Association of Community College Trustees (DC)

Alex Johnson, President, Cuyahoga Community College (OH)

Members

Helen Benjamin, Chancellor, Contra Costa Community College District (CA)

Gerardo E. de los Santos, President & CEO, League for Innovation in the Community College (AZ)

Kenneth L. Ender, President, William Rainey Harper College (IL)

Brenda Hellyer, Chancellor, San Jacinto College District (TX)

Steven Lee Johnson, President, Sinclair Community College (OH)

Cindy L. Miles, Chancellor, Grossmont–Cuyamaca Community College District (CA)

Lawrence A. Nespoli, President, New Jersey Council of County Colleges (NJ)

Angela Oriano, Executive Director, Texas Success Center, Texas Association of Community Colleges (TX)

Rod A. Risley, Executive Director, Phi Theta Kappa (MS)

Sanford C. "Sandy" Shugart, President, Valencia College (FL)

William E. Trueheart, President & CEO, Achieving the Dream, Inc. (MD)

Joshua Wyner, Executive Director, Aspen Institute, College Excellence Program (DC)

AACC Staff Liaisons

Kent Phillippe, Associate Vice President, Research & Student Success

Gail Schwartz, Senior Vice President, Innovative Learning & Student Success

Implementation Team 2: Reimagining Pathways for Students

Co-Chairs

Richard Carpenter, Chancellor, Lone Star College System (TX)

E. Ann McGee, President, Seminole State College of Florida (FL)

Members

George R. Boggs, President & CEO Emeritus, American Association of Community Colleges (CA)

Ned Doffoney, Chancellor, North Orange County Community College District (CA)

Mary S. Graham, President, Mississippi Gulf Coast Community College (MS)

Gregory J. Hamann, President, Linn-Benton Community College (OR)

Randall W. Hanna, Chancellor, Division of Florida Colleges (FL)

Brent Knight, President, Lansing Community College (MI)

Shaun L. McKay, President, Suffolk County Community College (NY)

Eloy Ortiz Oakley, Superintendent-President, Long Beach City College (CA)

DeRionne P. Pollard, President, Montgomery College (MD)

Jennifer Wimbish, President, Cedar Valley College (TX)

AACC Staff Liaisons

Charisse Bazin Ash, Associate Vice President, Human Resources

Mary Heiss, Associate Vice President, Strategic Initiatives

Implementation Team 3: Community College/K–12 Collaboration for College Readiness

Co-Chairs

Ken Atwater, President, Hillsborough Community College (FL)

Marie Foster Gnage, President, West Virginia University at Parkersburg (WV)

Richard M. Rhodes, President, Austin Community College (TX)

Members

Carole Berotte Joseph, President, Bronx Community College (NY)

Kevin E. Drumm, President, SUNY Broome Community College (NY)

Charlene M. Dukes, President, Prince George's Community College (MD)

Johanna Duncan-Poitier, Sr. Vice Chancellor for Community Colleges and the Education Pipeline, The State University of New York (NY)

Christine Johnson, Chancellor, Community College of Spokane (WA)

Kimberly O'Malley, Sr. Vice President of Research Services, Pearson Education (TX)

Robert Pura, President, Greenfield Community College (MA)

Anna Solley, President, Phoenix College (AZ)

Implementation Team 4: Developmental Education Redesign—Resources for Community Colleges

Co-Chairs

Myrtle E. B. Dorsey, Chancellor, St. Louis Community College District (MO)

Byron McClenney, Director (retired), Student Success Initiatives, The University of Texas at Austin (TX)

Members

Thomas Bailey, Professor of Economics and Education, Teachers College, Columbia University (NY)

Cynthia A. Bioteau, District President, Florida State College at Jacksonville (FL)

Richard Duran, President, Oxnard College (CA)

Rey Garcia, President & CEO, Texas Association of Community Colleges (TX)

Andrew C. Jones, Chancellor, Coast Community College District (CA)

Anne M. Kress, President, Monroe Community College (NY)

Sandra L. Kurtinitis, President, Community College of Baltimore County (MD)

Jackson N. Sasser, President, Santa Fe College (FL)

Philip Uri Treisman, Professor & Director, Charles A. Dana Center, University of Texas at Austin (TX)

Gregory Williams, President, Odessa College (TX)

AACC Staff Liaison

Kent Phillippe, Associate Vice President, Research & Student Success

Implementation Team 5: Closing the Skills Gap

Co-Chairs

Keith Bird, Sr. Policy Fellow for Workforce & Post Secondary Education, Corporation for a Skilled Workforce (SC)

James Jacobs, President, Macomb Community College (MI)

Members

Anthony P. Carnevale, Director & Research Professor, Georgetown University Center on Education & Workforce (DC)

Katharine Eneguess, President, White Mountains Community College (NH)

Edward L. Franklin, Executive Director (retired), Arkansas Association of Two-Year Colleges (AR)

Jana Kooi, President, Florida State College at Jacksonville-Open Campus (FL)

Andrew L. Meyer, Vice President, Workforce Development, League for Innovation in the Community College; Executive Director, Global Corporate College (AZ)

Camille Preus, President, Blue Mountain Community College (OR)

Van Ton-Quinlivan, Vice Chancellor, Workforce & Economic Development, California's Community Colleges (CA)

Betty Young, President, Houston Community College, Coleman College for Health Sciences (TX)

Federico Zaragoza, Vice Chancellor for Economic & Workforce Development, Alamo Community College District (TX)

P. Anthony Zeiss, President, Central Piedmont Community College (NC)

AACC Staff Liaison

Kathryn Jo Mannes, Senior Vice President, Workforce & Economic Development

Implementation Team 6: Policy and Advocacy Agenda for Reclaiming the American Dream

Co-Chairs

J. David Armstrong, Jr., President, Broward College (FL)

Rufus Glasper, Chancellor, Maricopa County Community College District (AZ)

Joe D. May, Chancellor, Dallas County Community College District (TX)

Members

Diane Bosak, Executive Director (former), Pennsylvania Commission for Community Colleges (PA)

J. Noah Brown, President & CEO, American Association of Community College Trustees (DC)

G. Edward Hughes, President, Gateway Community and Technical College (KY)

Jane A. Karas, President, Flathead Valley Community College (MT)

Scott Lay, President & CEO, Community College League of California (CA)

Paul E. Lingenfelter, President (retired), State Higher Education Executive Officers (CO)

Michael B. McCall, President, Kentucky Community and Technical College System (KY)

Marian Shivers, Dean, Leadership Institute, National Council on Black American Affairs (GA)

AACC Staff Liaisons

David Baime, Senior Vice President, Government Relations & Policy Analysis

Jim Hermes, Associate Vice President, Government Relations

Implementation Team 7: Redefining Institutional Roles and Functions

Co-Chairs

Daniel J. Phelan, President, Jackson College (MI)

Robert G. Templin, Jr., President, Northern Virginia Community College (VA)

Members

Chris Bustamante, President, Rio Salado College (AZ)

Erma Johnson Hadley, Chancellor, Tarrant County Community College (TX)

Audre Levy, President, Lone Star College-CyFair (TX)

Suzanne Miles, President-Community Campus (retired), Pima Community College (AZ)

Diana G. Oblinger, President & CEO, EDUCAUSE (DC)

Thomas J. Snyder, President, Ivy Tech Community College (IN)

Mick Starcevich, President, Kirkwood Community College (IA)

Steven L. VanAusdle, President, Walla Walla Community College (WA)

AACC Staff Liaison

Ramsay Johnson, Senior Vice President, Chief Operations & Financial Officer

Implementation Team 8: Accountability

Co-Chairs

Keith Miller, President, Greenville Technical College (SC)

Karen A. Stout, President, Montgomery County Community College (PA)

Members

Michael R. Chipps, President, Northeast Community College (NE)

Donald Doucette, Chancellor, Eastern Iowa Community College District (IA)

Katherine M. Johnson, President, Pasco-Hernando Community College (FL)

Timothy Nelson, President, Northwestern Michigan College (MI)

Shouan Pan, President, Mesa Community College (AZ)

R. Scott Ralls, President, North Carolina Community College System (NC)

Lori Sundberg, President, Carl Sandburg College (IL)

Millicent Valek, President, Brazosport College (TX)

Ronald Williams, Vice President (retired), College Board (DC)

AACC Staff Liaisons

David Baime, Senior Vice President, Government Relations & Policy Analysis

Kent Phillippe, Associate Vice President, Research & Student Success

Implementation Team 9: Faculty Engagement and Leadership Development

Co-Chairs

Stephen M. Curtis, President (retired), Community College of Philadelphia (PA)

Patricia Granados, President, Triton College (IL)

Jennifer Lara, Professor, Anne Arundel Community College (MD)

Rod A. Risley, Executive Director, Phi Theta Kappa (MS)

Members

J. Noah Brown, President & CEO, Association of Community College Trustees (DC)

Terry Calaway, President (retired), Johnson County Community College (KS)

Rita M. Cepeda, Chancellor, San Jose-Evergreen Community College District (CA)

Gerardo E. de los Santos, President & CEO, League for Innovation in the Community College (AZ)

René Díaz-Lefebvre, Professor of Psychology, Glendale Community College North (AZ)

M. J. Dolan, Executive Director, Iowa Association of Community College Trustees (IA)

Kathryn K. Eggleston, President, Richland College (TX)

Karla A. Fisher, Vice President of Academics, Butler Community College (KS)

Allatia Harris, President, San Jacinto College (TX)

Michael B. McCall, President, Kentucky Community and Technical College System (KY)

Laura Meeks, President, Eastern Gateway Community College (OH)

Brian Murphy, President, De Anza College (CA)

Richard Shrubb, President, Minnesota West Community and Technical College (MN)

Jianping Wang, Vice President for Academic Affairs, Ocean County College (NJ)

Joshua Wyner, Executive Director, Aspen Institute College Excellence Program (DC)

AACC Staff Liaisons

Angel Royal, Chief of Staff

Gail Schwartz, Senior Vice President, Innovative Learning & Student Success

Consultant to AACC President & CEO and Implementation Teams

Kay M. McClenney, Director, Center for Community College Student Engagement, Program in Higher Education Leadership, The University of Texas at Austin (TX)

AACC's 21st-Century Center

AACC's online 21st-Century Center is a repository of information that supports the work described in this *Implementation Guide*. AACC created this online center to help colleges achieve the goals set by the 21st-Century Commission on the Future of Community Colleges. At the center, college leaders, faculty and staff, and institutional partners will find additional examples of work underway, pertinent research, and news on the work of AACC and other organizations committed to reclaiming the American Dream through the work of community colleges. Visit the center at www.aacc21stcenturycenter.org.

Notes

[1] American Association of Community Colleges. (2013). Membership database.

[2] Organization for Economic Cooperation and Development. (2009). *Education at a glance, 2009: OECD indicators*. Paris: Author.

[3] DeNavas-Walt, C., Proctor, B. D., & Smith, J. C. (2011, September). *Income, poverty, and health insurance coverage in the United States: 2010* (P60-239). Washington, DC: U.S. Census Bureau.

[4] Associated Press. (2011, December 15). *Census data: Half of U.S. poor or low income*. Retrieved from www.cbsnews.com/8301-201_162-57343397/census-data-half-of-u.s.-poor-or-low-income/

[5] Carnevale, A. P., Smith, N., & Strohl, J. (2010). *Help wanted: Projections of jobs and education requirements*. Washington, DC: Georgetown University, Center on Education and the Workforce.

[6] Berkner, L., & Choy, S. (2008). *Descriptive summary of 2003–04 beginning postsecondary students: Three years later* (NCES 2008-174). Washington, DC: National Center for Education Statistics, Institute of Education Sciences, U.S. Department of Education. Retrieved from www.nces.ed.gov/pubs2008/2008174.pdf

[7] Radford, A. W., Berkner, L., Wheeless, S. C., & Shepherd, B. (2010). *Persistence and attainment of 2003–04 beginning postsecondary students: After 6 years* (NCES 2011-151). Washington, DC: National Center for Educational Statistics. Retrieved from www.nces.ed.gov/pubs2011/2011151.pdf